Behind Walls & Glass

poems by

Mahtem Shiferraw

Finishing Line Press
Georgetown, Kentucky

Behind Walls & Glass

ACKNOWLEDGMENTS

A heartfelt thank you to those who contributed to the realization of this chapbook; to my family, my friends and fellow writers. A big thank you to Medhanie Zeleke for giving the book a stunning visual. Thank you also to Sarah Maclay for her kind words. Thank you to Finishing Line Press for giving my work a proper home.

Editor: Christen Kincaid

Cover Art: Medhanie Zeleke

Author Photo: Mahtem Shiferraw

Cover Design: Elizabeth Maines

Printed in the USA on acid-free paper.
Order online: www.finishinglinepress.com
          also available on amazon.com

Author inquiries and mail orders:
Finishing Line Press
P. O. Box 1626
Georgetown, Kentucky 40324
U. S. A.

Table of Contents

Having little or no
mouth in my soul
I find myself
knocking
to get to sea.

This is my
sword;

there is nothing
but the ocean
with me.

Like a lover's quarrel

It begins on a moonless night
like any other;

see how I am sitting on the top bunk
waiting for star lights to exhale
their ghostly presence?

That is where I am, mostly,
among the presence of ghosts
and though I am only twelve

I am convinced I am one too
because how else can I explain

this removal, this detachment,
a disassembling of selves

heads rested on blue walls
razor sharp nails sinking into white pillows,

how to explain this conflict

continuous, intimate
like a lover's quarrel

showing up in the middle of the night
in the middle of a night terror
in the middle of a thought?

Longing

I used to long for the sea
before I even knew what it was

before I knew
how cruel water can be
in its slippery nature, its swallowing texture

how daunting, how amorous and
bewitching, how it knew exactly my name

and mine only

waves calling my name like it was a secret
a whisper I could only hear

and I thought,

the sea longs for me
as I long for its embrace.

Because I write poems in Italian ...

I like words like *sponda*, and *spiaggia*, and *spume*

words that fill my mouth
with the sound of being
the sound of living.

I also know
words like *guerra* and *terra*, words that

roll my tongue
sleep in its bed
find solace in memories of memories,

roots for my loves
and my fears.

Water

It is Autumn
when I first see it:

the light of knitted rain
the smell of wet mud
water in the shoes.

Is this water the same
as any water? As the water
that wants to kill me?

Between the living & the dying

I often think of skulls –

how they look so lonely
without their tissue, their flesh,
vibrant skin, how they are nothing

without the body attached to them

and yet

here they are
belonging to no one
belonging to a state of dreams
belonging to the dead
and the living at the same time.

But what about
those of us who are between
the living and the dying?

Where do our skulls
belong?

The First Time
(it must be in 9th grade)

We are on the third floor
and I go out the window

the thrill of death almost palpable

what if I jump, I ask.
Amayes holds my hand.

Then you would be dead, he says.

It's so simple, so terrifying.

I don't jump;

I've always despised
uncomplicated things anyway.

The Tree of Stories

What of fire?

Doesn't it consume you
with the appetite of a lover too?

Or does it approach fast
with the spear of the enemy?

I want to hold it in my hands
kiss its flames
dip my hair into that succulent orange

all the colors I want to use for my suicide are there –

a tender blue, the shadow of gray, the blood of red,
the purple of plum, the yellow of the sun, the white of ghosts;

I think of it like this:
I will die multi-chromatic.

But what about
the blackness of it all?

The burning,
the charcoal body,
the smell of smoke?

This is not it, this is not *how* I want it to happen;

so instead I burn
entire notebooks filled with poems, stories
I've written at night

and characters melt quickly, pages devoured
one after the other, and what is left is

the ash of sorrow
the ash of poetry,

and I dig a hole in the garden
by joyous *adey abeba*, and plant

the ashes of dead stories and dead poems inside
and weep slowly, quietly.

Years later
when a young tree appears
I think of it as
the tree of my stories,
and that is how I tell it:

there is a tree of stories in my garden
and it does not want to be disturbed
because death hangs loosely from its branches
and its leaves are a shade darker than the night
and it bears no fruit, no characters, no people,
no plots, it bears no names,

the tree of my stories
the tree of my deaths.

On Freedom & Doubt

There are things I like
about her; not many

but enough to keep us both
in one body.

We stay up at night
writing letters to Sgroi Libertá;

"Carissima Nonna,
oggi la luna é crudele, il sole scomosso
la terra buia, in sangue evaso."

It is the same litany
as ever before –

Where is this freedom you speak of?
Why is there so much doubt in me?

And the answer comes
in the shape of a poem;

la poesia é la libertá

poetry is the freedom you seek
and doubt is what you do with it

but I never stop thinking of Leopardi
and *il dolce naufragar*

and so poetry must be water
because I'm already longing for it

a disquieted longing without solace.

Death by Trains

I am in Italy
in the hands of a boy
when I contemplate suicide by trains again;

it is not the first time
I find myself attracted
to their speed, their light, their lightning bolt.

I ask the same question:

what if I jump?

He says, *not now,*
but he means, *not here.*

I want to say,
I need accomplices
to hold *her* down;

she is unafraid

of things moving, things stagnant, things poised
things sharp, things enveloping, things tall
things suffocating, things undead, things numb.

I am afraid
of everything.

Mostly of the way I keep thinking
about skulls, and the merciful beheading
of chickens, and the lost songs of goat herders

and of myself.

Whomever we are.

When Men Come

She hides a knife
under the pillow

because she fears for us.

She says, when men come
we will plunge the blade
upon their flesh, see our
reflection in this
before they are silenced.

I say, when men come
we will plunge the blade
upon ourselves.

It is an argument
we cannot get away from,

an exhaustion
that drives us apart.

The Art of Sorrow

There are moments
of despair, but of
tenderness too.

Don't you know how
long it takes

to muster the art of sorrow?

How secretive melancholy can be
if left alone?

This is what keeps us going:

the heart, the ghosts, the blackness,
the colors, the sunset, the moon, the
laughter of hyenas, the stories, the stories,
always the stories, the eyes of strangers,
the memory of grandfathers. And poetry.

It always comes back
to poetry, to freedom.

To My Assailant

I don't know why
you are who you are

you do what you do

as ordinary as you are
even boring, maybe

as nice as you are

I don't know where
to place this monster
of you, this piece you left

the one you took of me
the ones you left on my other half
the ones you left on others.

I don't know why
you look the way you do

why you don't come
with a warning sign,
the curse of Ishmael on your forehead.

I don't know how
you have a mother as you do

how extraordinary you must be
to her fearful heart, her longing soul.

I don't know because

these things do not make sense
(they ought not to).

But I know this:

one day I will forgive you
because I must
because there are too many shattered selves
to contain in one body.

One day, I must.

Black & Blue

The first time we see the ocean
it is coated in black
and blue.

I see the black
she sees the blue.

It's nighttime, and we can only hear it:
a slight rumbling, crushing of waves
into voiceless sands.

We go back
to collect pebbles, polish their smooth faces
kiss their forehead
and store them in a clear vase

drenched in water
as they were meant to be.

It is a sign:

a piece of the ocean
in the intimacy of a closed space;

a quenching for the longing
we have endured for so long.

Neither Here, Nor There

A red towel
hangs by the door

but it wants to be purple.

This is what we do
all the time, this is our thing:

we quarrel because we are not the same
but we do it with the tenacity of belonging
to the same being, inhabiting the same body.

We walk clueless
and do not notice others staring
the nail polish: burgundy on one hand
dark blue on the other.

It is a thing, here.

One of us speaks
and her voice is quiet,
the other dissents
and she is loud.

But what splits us most:

ruthless thoughts, thousands at a time
demanding space, & attention, & more sorrow
demanding to be articulated, given life
into this world.

But how do you articulate
this?

We are neither here
nor there

entangled
in a slow process
of agony

that does not let us be.

Because the Body

does not break at sight

I feed it sweets, because the world
is sour in my mouth.

The Fourth Suicide

We stand tall
above a cliff;

palm trees soaring
over wooden benches.

It does not smell of death
but of Spring, and something
romantic.

Lovers hold hands, kiss
through the sunset, murmur
secrets full of promise.

But we are as alone
as we'll ever be.

It is not the fear of dying
that keeps us from jumping;

it is the fear of *not* dying
after such courageous attempt.

It is the fear
of surviving.

Letters of Love

I write letters to a woman I don't know
because she sends me poetry;

I tell her how alone I am
yet how tiring to sustain myself
all by myself.

She might not know me
but she knows *this* –

how solitary the act of writing is,
the act of dying, teeth to dirt, skull
to skull, bones to ash.

She must know *this*
because why else would she write back?

I write of everything
and of nothing

but you don't need words
to know *this*

only eyes, and a tongue wet with fear.

Questions for Your Selves

It must be something
about your art.

Why are your poems
so sad?

Were you someone else
in another life?

And who told you
to nest such sorrow in your bones?

Don't you know better?

Can't you see your mother's eyes
grieving in eternity?

You have a mother too
and you must be extraordinary too

and you must be longed for too.

Because why else
would you still be here?

Unbroken

You think of your brother often.
You say, he would've understood

because he must, because he is
exactly like you, or you like him

either way, he would understand
what you can't even articulate.

After all, didn't you see white ghosts
around him too, adorning his dreadlocks
like garlands, hushing him to sleep?

Didn't you hear it in his voice, his modesty,
his optimism, his fragility?

He is strong
because he has to be

because he is exposed –

his wounds too raw
his sorrow too new
his spirit unbroken.

Behind Walls & Glass

There are many places
where you can hide

but none are safe
for you to call home.

This is a land that fed you
meat and frozen vegetables

a land that calls you
alien and immigrant

a land that defines your self-worth
by the color of your skin

a land where your language
is soundless, asleep.

How can this be home?

Isn't that a place
where you can be who you want to be

where meat comes from goat herders
where papayas are the size of cats
where God is only God
where black & brown & white
are only colors

where you fall, and a flower blossoms
in your name

where you are not asked
if you have a nickname
if you were colonized
if your ancestors were tied & sold
to the ferrous hearts of sea merchants

if you know anyone else in the entire continent
if you were a child soldier
if you have starved.

This is not it.
This is the place to hide

behind walls & glass
behind fake accents and quick smiles
behind designer clothes
& fancy cars
& lavish trips
& dancing
& nightclubs
& short shorts
& scorned boys who want to claim your body
before you know it is yours.

This is
your hiding place:

tell no one and you'll be safe.

The Shape of Night Shadows

When you think of children
don't think of them as children,

instead

think of them as characters;
see how one's laughter
catches your ear, the other's cry
awakens something unworldly in you.

You were once a child too:

lost in a sea of characters not your own,
lost in a world where books take the shape
of night shadows, a world where
you choose and pick
who to love, who to kill.

What books don't tell you:
the other world
you belong in;

only your body knows it.

Your mind is where
you left it once,

by the side streets
of unwritten bodies

thoughts half bitten, half bleeding,

where only a weeping pen
sets you free.

And when you write,
remember this:

the shape of your night shadows
is the gateway to somebody else's,
a place they'll call home.

The Fifth Time

Around the fifth time
Noel & Delina enter my life;
they are both eight.

They love me
for reasons I cannot understand

and I search for answers
in their bright eyes
their sunny smiles,

but nothing.

I take them to the beach
and they hold my hand

and I am humbled, humbled to have them,
humbled to have been loved
so freely.

But I am no one, I think.

And yet, here they were
thinking I am someone
thinking I am someone special.

How can this be?
How can someone like me
be loved so dearly?

They smile and the waters open
like blossoming flowers
and winds dance
and the sand is softer again.

The same waters
that will close on me
the same winds
that will choke me
the same sand
that swallows me whole.

This must be
love too.

A List

There is a time
when I am angry at God
and yet He is so gentle
I succumb to His ways.

I want to tell Him
I don't think of *this* as a sin
because how can it be
when I am reduced to
being split in half?

I want to know
what He wants from me –
though I am not ready to hear it.

I don't want to be wanted
or loved
or mourned for;

I want to disappear
go to sleep
and never wake up.

I want this
because I already know
everything else there is to know
about this world.

I want this mostly
not because of the sorrow – which is sickening,
but because I am tired.

What I will miss most?

I make a list,
like I always do
when I have errands to run;

my father's laughter
my mother's voice
my siblings
my friends

I will also miss

the wind in my face
the smell of the ocean
waking up to an empty sky;

I will miss most
my cities, lands I claimed
without their knowing,

my Asmara, my city of birth
my Addis Ababa, the flower of my face
my Rome, the love of my poetry
my San Francisco, the artist of me;

I will miss rain, and morning
and evenings
and warm afternoons

and *gelato alla stracciatella*
and *panini*, and writing poetry
and reading
and inhabiting a world
not my own.

I will miss me
in here.

But in here
is all gray now:

all I see
is myself
and she does not
look back.

Resemblance

At some point
you will be asked

if your hair can be touched;

even though it's not in a fro anymore
even though your hairline has receded
from so much pulling
even though your hair is attached
to your head

and your head
to your body
and your body
to your spirit

even though there are places
a hand will reach
after touching your hair,
even though it is unsought,
unwarranted, even though
it shouldn't be there.

Your mane
is not only yours
it is your body's;

each single strand
accounted for.

What you should know is this:
when stranger's hands reach for your body,
(any part of your body):

never forget
you are a resemblance
of the divine;

no hand shall tarnish
the value of your life.

The Body of Punishments

You crave the unknown
like your body craves punishment;

and there are different flavors for it.

A father throwing
the sleeping body of his daughter
down the stairs

the hands of a homeless man struck down
with a silent bullet

the corpses of chairs and tables
thrown against the walls

a belt's peeled skin
because of too many lashings

the body left untouched
after so much fumbling.

It is easier
to distance yourself
from it all, anything that can numb
this grayness out of you.

But let us help you remember
what this body *wants* to crave:

sunbathing in the Spring
a soft kiss on the throat
tickling hair in the back of the neck
ocean water under the feet
rain all over its skin.

This body of punishments
wants to be remembered
for what it could have been:

a home for the displaced.

Interplay

She shows up in your poems
she shows up in your dreams

he shows up in your art.

She speaks to you
she waits for you

he remains a shadow.

She argues with you
she laughs with you

he remains a shadow.

She cries with you
she looks for you

he remains a shadow.

She sleeps with you
she whispers to you

he is a walking shadow.

She calls your name
he calls your name.

She comes close to you
he comes closer.

You fall
and he catches both of you.

You are now shadows too.

Thoughts on Melancholia

There is beauty in sadness
because it takes courage to remain in sorrow;

look how flowers blossom – red, pink, yellow,
colors as numerous as the stars,
and we smell their aroma
inhale their beauty

but wait for them to sag, skin rotten
petals torn, leaves falling
colorless too soon

then we take our eyes away
because they remind us
how imminent death & dying are
how quick to claim those unprepared
how unforgiving in their power.

What we fear most
is not being gone, or dying a slow death,
or a quick one, no, it is all

in how we are remembered
or forgotten.

Who will recall my name, the sound of
my voice, the grace of my walk, the light
in my talk?

Who will willfully acknowledge
the grief in my heart, the joy in my sorrow,
the shine in my craft, my hope in tomorrow?

And who will, remembering these
& me
& the memory of me

who will dare say
I loved thee like a summer's day?

Only poems dare to claim
the dead, the dying, the undying
and the willfully melancholic.

Love Is to Love Is to Lust as to Lure

Love is to love as in:

the lion's jaw
locked into
the belly of the doe

the warm bleeding heart.

Or as in:

a woman's unclaimed body
explored by others
nakedness even in clothes

and

her lust hanging like white honey
between her breasts
a warmth so articulate
needless for words, for approval.

Also, as in:

the luring promises
to children
and the children
in adult bodies.

But mostly, it is about
something taken
a fleeting moment
a joy
an innocence

something as old as the soul
and yet as new as the breath

something we didn't know we had
until it is lost.

Mahtem Shiferraw is a poet and visual artist who grew up in Ethiopia and Eritrea. Her work has been published in *Callaloo, The Bitter Oleander Press, Cactus Heart Press, Luna Luna Magazine, The 2River View* and elsewhere. She is the recipient of the 2015 Sillerman First Book Prize for African Poets and her first full length collection, *FUCHSIA*, is forthcoming from the University of Nebraska Press. She holds an MFA in Creative Writing from Vermont College of Fine Arts.